The GROSS AND GOOFY Body

Pump It Up!

The Secrets of the Heart and Blood

By Melissa Stewart

Illustrated by Janet Hamlin

mc Marshall Cavendish
Benchmark
New York

This book was made possible,

in part, by a grant from the

Society of Children's Book Writers and Illustrators.

Marshall Cavendish Benchmark
99 White Plains Road
Tarrytown, NY 10591-5502
www.marshallcavendish.us

Stewart, Melissa.
Pump it up! : the secrets of the heart and blood / by Melissa Stewart.
p. cm. — (The gross and goofy body)
Includes index.
Summary: "Provides comprehensive information on the role the heart plays
in the body science of humans and animals"—Provided by publisher.
ISBN 978-0-7614-4164-9
1. Heart—Juvenile literature. 2. Blood—Juvenile literature. I. Title.
QP111.6.S74 2010
612.1'7—dc22
2008033552

Photo research by Tracey Engel

Cover photo: © Ingram Publishing (Superstock Limited)/Alamy

The photographs in this book are used by permission and through the courtesy of:
Alamy: Joe McDonald, 5 (bottom); isobel flynn, 9; Rob Walls, 17; Nigel Cattlin, 18; foodfolio, 22.
PHOTOTAKE Inc., 28; Sara Zinelli, 30; Deco, 40 (right). *Corbis:* Ruben Sprich/Reuters, 10; Jose Luis
Pelaez, Inc., 16; Tracy Kahn, 29 (bottom); Brandon D. Cole, 35 (bottom); Ron Boardman, Frank Lane
Picture Agency, 37. Digital Railroad: Olivier Robin, 27. *Getty Images:* Frank Greenaway, 7; Dr. Kessel &
Dr. Kardon/Tissues & Organs, 26; Rebecca Emery, 29 (top); Dr. Dennis Kunkel, 38 (right). iStockphoto:
Felix Möckel, 8. *Minden Pictures:* Chris Newbert, 36. *Photo Researchers, Inc.:* Tom McHugh, 5 (top);
J. Bavosi, 24; Biophoto Associates, 32 (left); St Bartholomew's Hospital, 32 (right); Science Source, 33;
Friedrich Saurer, 35 (top); Andrew Paul Leonard, 38 (left); Simon Fraser, 40 (left).

Editor: Joy Bean
Publisher: Michelle Bisson
Art Director: Anahid Hamparian
Series Designer: Daniel Roode

Printed in Malaysia

1 3 5 6 4 2

CONTENTS

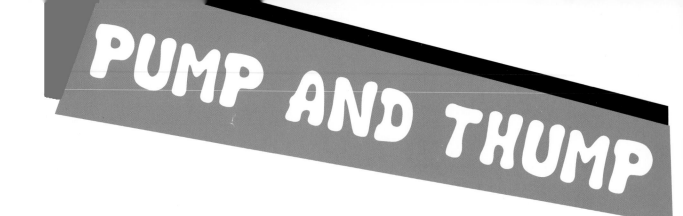

You can't cut open your chest and a take look at your heart. You'd make a bloody mess. And boy, would it hurt! But it's easy to feel your heart doing its job.

Place two fingers on either side of your neck and push gently against your throat. Feel that steady throbbing under your skin? That's your **pulse**. You feel a thump each time your heart beats.

Your heart is a muscle about the size of your fist. It is an **organ** that is strong enough to pump more than 1,500 gallons (5,678 liters) of blood every day, and it never takes a break. Good thing, too—your life depends on it. You'll be amazed at all the ways a heart and blood make life better for you—and for other animals, too.

When a spider **molts**, or sheds its skin, its heart pumps extra blood into the front of its body. The blood pushes on the old skin until it cracks open.

A Burmese python needs extra pumping power to digest large **prey**. Luckily, its heart can bulk up 40 percent in just two days.

In winter, a wood frog's heart stops beating—for weeks. But the little leaper isn't dead. The warm days of spring will jump-start its heart.

YOUR HARDWORKING HEART

You need your stomach to **digest,** or break down, food. You need your lungs to take in air. But what about your heart? Why is pumping blood so important?

Your blood is like an express-mail worker. It makes deliveries and pickups all day long.

As blood flows past your **small intestine**, it picks up tiny bits of digested food and delivers the **nutrients** to all of your cells.

As blood passes through your lungs, it collects the **oxygen** you breathe in and carries it to every single cell in your body. It also transports **carbon dioxide** and other waste materials away from your cells.

Your hardworking heart's contraction action also delivers chemical messengers called **hormones**, and it shuttles germ-fighting cells from one battle to the next.

Suck It Up !

Why do leeches, ticks, vampire bats, and female mosquitoes feast on blood? Because it's full of nutrients. Most people try to stay away from blood-sucking creatures, but leeches aren't all bad. When someone loses a finger or toe in an accident, a surgeon sews it back on. Sometimes a doctor places leeches on wounds. Their sucking action helps get the patient's blood flowing.

WARMING UP, COOLING DOWN

What do pigs and parrots, eagles and elephants all have in common? They're **warm-blooded** animals. Their body temperature stays the same no matter how cold or warm it is around them. Humans are warm-blooded, too.

Your body temperature is usually about 98.6 degrees Fahrenheit (37 degrees Celsius). When the air around you is hotter or colder, many parts of your body—including your heart and your blood—work together to warm you up or cool you down.

Too hot? Your heart pumps extra blood toward your skin, making you sweat. The heat escapes into the air, and your body starts to cool off.

Got a chill? Your heart pumps very little blood to your skin. That helps you hold on to your precious body heat.

Beating the Heat

When an elephant feels hot, it flaps its ears. That releases heat from the blood flowing through them. Then the blood travels to the rest of the elephant's body and cools it off.

A dog does the same thing with its tongue. When a dog pants, its spit **evaporates**, or turns into a gas that rises into the air. As the dog's tongue cools down, so does the blood inside it. Then the dog's heart pumps the cooled blood throughout its body.

RATE AND RHYTHM

The last time you went to the doctor's office, a nurse probably placed two fingers on the inside of your wrist and looked at his or her watch. The nurse was checking your pulse rate. It's a quick way to tell how well your heart is working.

Most of the time, your heart beats about eighty or ninety times a minute. People who exercise a lot have lower heart rates. The hearts of some Olympic athletes beat just thirty times a minute.

To check your heart rate, sit quietly in a chair. Find your pulse on your neck or your wrist. Then use a watch with a second hand to count how many thumps you feel in a minute.

Want to know how many times your heart beats in an hour? Just multiply by sixty minutes. Multiply that answer by twenty-four hours to find out how many times your heart beats each day.

This milk jug contains 1 gallon (3.8 liters) of liquid. Your heart can pump that amount of liquid in just twenty seconds.

The Beat Goes On

Your heart keeps on pumping day and night, year after year. During your lifetime, it will beat about 3 billion times and pump about 100 million gallons (379 million l) of blood through your body.

IS BIGGER BETTER?

Believe it or not, size makes a big difference when it comes to heart rate. Scientists have measured the heart rates of many different **mammals** and a few birds, too. What did they learn? On average, the bigger an animal is, the slower its heart beats.

And that's not all. An animal's size and heart rate usually determine how long it lives. Scientists discovered that most animal hearts have an upper limit of about 1.5 billion beats. A mouse's heart beats very quickly, so it uses up its 1.5 billion beats in just a couple of years. But an elephant's slow-beating heart can keep on pumping for sixty years.

People are smaller than elephants, so why do we live even longer? Because we have big brains. We use them to stay safe, clean, well fed, and healthy. Our lives are easier, so we can live longer.

Animal	Heart Rate (bpm)	Average Life Span (years)
Hummingbird	1,200	1
Mouse	700	2 to 3
Hamster	450	3 to 5
Hedgehog	300	4 to 7
Chicken	275	5 to 8
Rabbit	205	6 to 8
Monkey	190	25
Cat	150	15
Small dog	100	12
Large dog	75	10
Pig	70	15
Cow	65	20
Giraffe	65	25
Elephant	30	60
Whale	20	80

Fight or Flight

No matter how big or small an animal is, its heart beats faster when it feels scared or excited. That's because the animal's body is getting ready to protect itself. When an animal runs away from or attacks an enemy, its muscles need more oxygen-rich blood than usual.

Your heart is a double pump with four chambers—two **atria** on top and two **ventricles** below them. And each heartbeat is made up of two contractions. Both of your atria fill with blood at the same time, but from different places. They contract gently to move blood down into your ventricles. Then your ventricles contract powerfully to propel blood to your lungs and throughout your body.

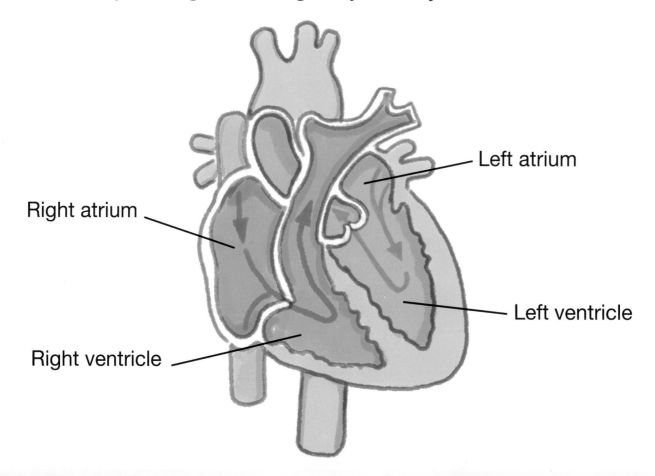

Right atrium

Left atrium

Right ventricle

Left ventricle

Blood from the body enters your heart's right atrium. It contains very little oxygen, but it's full of carbon dioxide.

As your heart muscle contracts, blood gushes into your right ventricle. Less than half a second later, your heart contracts again. Blood surges into a large **blood vessel** that carries it to your lungs.

As the blood travels through your lungs, it picks up a fresh supply of oxygen. It also gets rid of carbon dioxide. Then it flows back to your heart and enters the left atrium.

When your heart contracts, it squeezes the blood into your left ventricle. And when it contracts again, blood bursts out of your heart and travels to the rest of your body.

Did You Know?

Blood makes up about 7 percent of your body's total weight. So if you weigh 100 pounds (45 kilograms), the 6 quarts (5.7 l) of blood circulating through your body weigh about 7 pounds (3 kg).

SOOTHING SOUNDS

Lub-dub, lub-dub. That's the soothing sound of your heart at work. Doctors can hear it when they place a **stethoscope** on your chest.

You might think it's the noise your heart muscle makes each time it contracts. But guess again. It's really the sound of valves inside your heart slamming shut after each contraction—just like tiny doors. By opening and closing at just the right time, the valves keep blood flowing in the right direction.

After your heart pumps blood from your atria into your ventricles, valves between them slap together. *Lub.* And after blood gushes up and out of your ventricles, two more valves slam closed. *Dub.* They stop blood from draining back into your heart.

Pumping Power

Each beat of your heart pumps about 5 tablespoons (74 milliliters) of blood into your blood vessels. Most of the time, your heart sends out about 2.5 gallons (9.5 l) of blood per minute. But when you exercise, your heart picks up its pace. At top speed it can pump up to 20 gallons (76 l) per minute.

OTHER KINDS OF HEARTS

Most animals have hearts, but they don't all look like yours, and they don't all work in the same way.

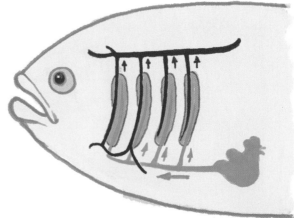

An earthworm has five short, thick tubes just behind its head. Some scientists call them hearts. They force blood into two long, thin blood vessels that carry blood throughout the worm's body.

A fish's heart looks more like yours, but it has only one atrium and one ventricle. Each time the ventricle contracts, it pushes blood into the fish's **gills**. After the blood picks up oxygen and gets rid of carbon dioxide, it flows slowly through the rest of the fish's body.

A frog's heart has two atria and one ventricle. Blood from the body enters the right atrium. It has very little oxygen. Blood from the lungs enters the left atrium. It is full of oxygen. Some of the blood mixes in the ventricle, but the frog's cells still get enough oxygen to survive.

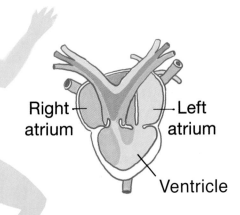

Right atrium

Left atrium

Ventricle

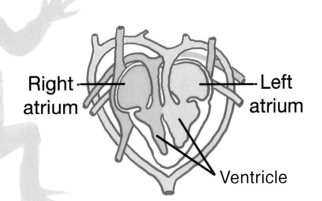

Right atrium

Left atrium

Ventricle

Like frogs, most lizards and snakes have one ventricle. A partial wall inside the ventricle helps keep blood with lots of oxygen separate from blood with very little oxygen.

HACKING OUT HEARTS

Think life's hard today? At least you don't have to worry about someone slicing open your chest and ripping out your heart while it's still beating. In the 1400s and early 1500s, twenty thousand people a year died that way in central Mexico. And many of them considered it an honor!

The ancient Aztecs thought hearts were magical—especially the young, pure hearts of children. They believed the heart contained the spirit that gives life. After removing a person's heart, Aztec priests mixed it with blood, peanuts, chocolate, and hot peppers. Then they ate it. Ew! Disgusting!

Why did the priests carry out such a gross and grisly ritual? To please their gods. They thought human sacrifices would bring just the right amount of sunshine and rain for their crops. They also hoped the sacrifices would prevent earthquakes and other natural disasters.

Yummy in Your Tummy

In some cultures, people enjoy eating the hearts of cows, sheep, and pigs. And you can find chicken hearts in some North American grocery stores. Some people say the mighty muscle tastes like a nice, juicy steak, but you might want to stick with PB&J.

Aztecs weren't the only ancient people fascinated by the human heart. For thousands of years, people all over the world have been curious about the mysterious mass of muscle in the center of the chest. And each ancient culture had its own ideas about the heart's role in the body.

Today, we know exactly what the heart does—and doesn't—do. But that doesn't stop us from talking about broken hearts or giving heart-shaped boxes of candy to our loved ones on Valentine's Day.

4000 B.C.E. to 1397 C.E. Ancient India
People believed the heart was the center of thinking and **consciousness**.

3100 B.C.E. to 31 B.C.E. Ancient Egypt
People believed the heart was the center of feelings and intelligence.

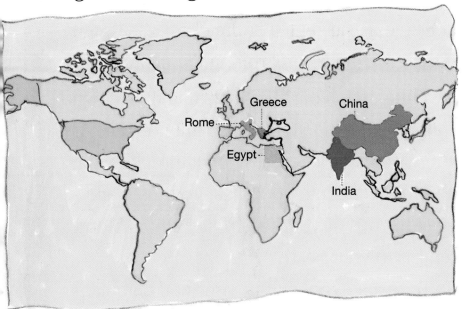

2000 B.C.E. to 1644 C.E. Ancient China
People believed the heart was the center of happiness.

1100 B.C.E. to 146 B.C.E. Ancient Greece
People believed the heart was the seat of the spirit.

146 B.C.E. to 476 C.E. Ancient Rome
People believed the heart was the center of feelings.

Who Was Valentine?

Valentine's Day is named after a priest who lived about eight hundred years ago. He secretly married Roman soldiers and their sweethearts even though it was against the law. After Valentine was captured and thrown in jail, he fell in love with the guard's blind daughter. He sent her heart-shaped love notes signed "from your Valentine." Today, people send more than 900 million valentines to their loved ones every February 14.

BLOOD ON THE MOVE

After oxygen-rich blood surges out of your heart's left ventricle, it begins a long journey to the far corners of your body. Imagine it traveling up to your shoulders and then down your arms. Or up your neck and into your brain. Some of it courses down through your **abdomen** and into your legs, your feet, and even the tips of your toes. Then all the blood returns to your heart.

To reach every cell in your body, your blood travels through nearly 60,000 miles (96,560 kilometers) of blood vessels. They make up your **circulatory system**.

Some blood vessels are as thick as your thumb. Others are much thinner than a strand of hair. If all of your blood vessels were placed end to end, they'd circle the world almost two and a half times. Now that's incredible!

Laughter Really Is the Best Medicine

Want to stay healthy? Have a good laugh—and that's no joke. When you laugh, giggle, or snort, your body releases a chemical that relaxes your blood vessels. And when vessels relax, more blood can flow through them. That means your cells get more of the oxygen and nutrients they need to do their jobs.

ROUND AND ROUND

As blood circles through your body, it moves through three kinds of blood vessels. First, it whizzes through your **arteries**, traveling at 1 foot (0.3 meters) per second. But then it puts on the brakes as it squeezes through your superslender **capillaries**.

Capillaries make up about 99 percent of your circulatory system—and it's a good thing, too. Something very important happens inside these tiny transport tubes. It's where oxygen from your lungs and nutrients from your intestines move out of your blood and into your cells. At the same time, carbon dioxide and other wastes move out of your cells and into your blood.

Red blood cells squeeze through a capillary in this view through a microscope.

Finally, your blood slowly slogs its way back to your heart through your **veins**. You may never catch a glimpse of your arteries or your capillaries, but it's easy to see your veins. Just look for blue lines under the skin on your hands and arms.

Spooky-Eyed

Ever taken a picture of a friend at night? If your camera's flash went off, your friend's eyes probably looked red in the photo. That crazy color shows up when light from the flash bounces off all the capillaries at the back of your friend's eyes.

A FLOOD OF BLOOD

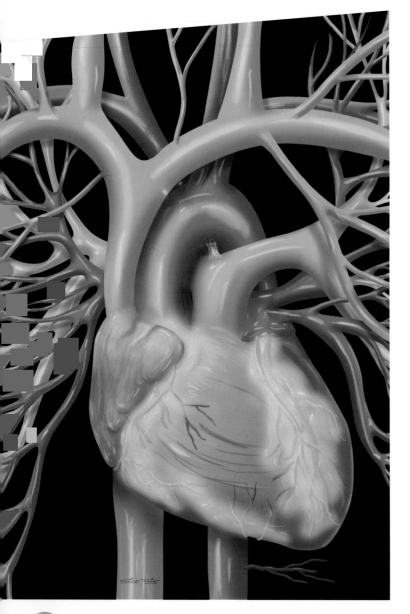

In most parts of your body, your arteries lie below your veins. And that's no accident. Cutting a vein is usually no big deal, but slicing open an artery can be a matter of life and death.

The blood in your arteries is under a lot of pressure from your pounding heart. Cut an artery open, and blood would gush out. But your heart's thumping and throbbing has less effect on your veins. Blood trickles out of them much more slowly. So the positioning of your blood vessels helps you survive.

This artwork shows arteries (red) and veins (blue and purple) surrounding the heart.

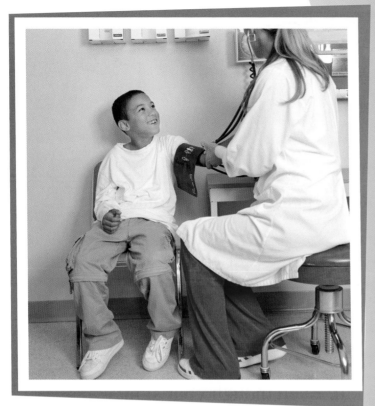

Under Pressure

The last time you went to the doctor's office, a nurse probably put a cuff around your arm and inflated it by squeezing a plastic ball attached to a tube. The nurse was checking your **blood pressure**—the force of the blood pushing against your artery walls. It's a quick way to determine how hard your heart is working.

Blood pressure is always given as two numbers, such as 110/70. The first number is the force of blood pushing against your artery walls when your heart muscle contracts. The second number is the force of blood pushing against your artery walls when your heart relaxes.

GOT THE BLUES?

What's the first thing you notice when you look at blood? It's color, of course. The more oxygen your blood contains, the redder it looks.

So if blood is red, why do your veins look blue? Well, it's complicated. The blood inside your veins is low in oxygen. So it isn't bright red. It's a dark purplish red.

You're seeing that blood through the wall of a blood vessel and several layers of skin. Even though your skin and vessel walls are transparent, they aren't colorless. When all their colors combine, you see blue.

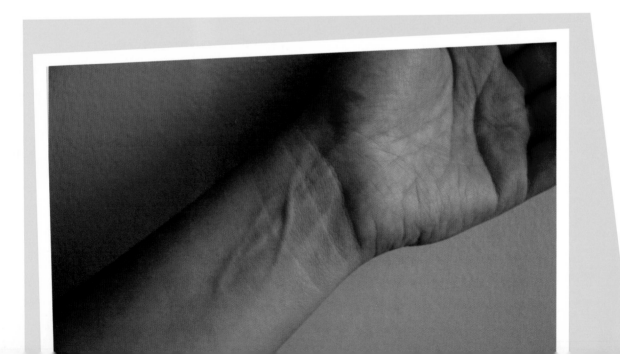

Quick Change

Why does the blood trickling out of a cut vein look bright red? Because the moment the dark purplish blood hits the air, it mixes with oxygen and changes color.

Blue Bloods

In the 1800s, people in Europe began calling upper-class citizens "blue bloods." At the time, most people were poor farmers who spent many hours tending crops. As the sun tanned their skin, their veins looked less and less blue. But the royal family and nobility stayed out of the sun. Because their skin was so pale, their blue veins really stood out.

THE LIQUID OF LIFE

Why do some people call blood "the liquid of life"? Because it contains so many important ingredients.

A pale yellow liquid called **plasma** makes up about 55 percent of your blood. Plasma's main ingredient is water, but it also contains salts, nutrients, hormones, and waste products from your cells.

Blood has two important kinds of cells. **Red blood cells (RCBs)** give your blood its color. They also pick up oxygen in your lungs and deliver it to all the cells in your body.

White blood cells (WBCs) fight the bacteria and viruses that make you sick. Blood also contains **platelets,** which are broken bits and pieces of cells. When you get a cut, they help stop the bleeding.

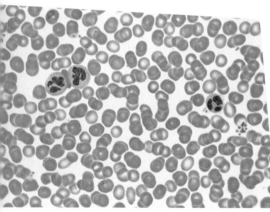

Blood, as seen under a microscope.

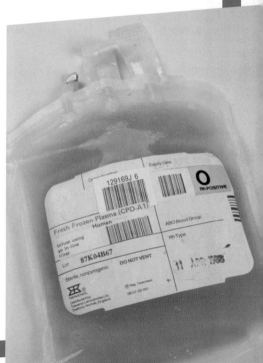

This transfusion bag contains plasma but no blood cells.

Where's the Blood?

Right now, your body contains about 6 quarts (5.7 l) of blood. About 24 percent of that blood is in your arteries. About 66 percent is in your veins, and about 10 percent is in your capillaries.

Red blood cells (in red), white blood cells (yellowish), and platelets (green) make up blood cells.

GRAB AND GO

Red blood cells (RBCs) look like tiny deflated basketballs. As they bob and bounce through your lungs, they pick up the fresh oxygen **molecules** that you've just breathed in.

The oxygen grabs onto a **protein** called **hemoglobin**—just like a little kid getting a piggyback ride. Every RBC contains about 270 million molecules of hemoglobin, and each one can carry its own oxygen molecule.

As your blood flows past all the cells in your body, the oxygen molecules break away from their hemoglobin partners and move into your cells. Then the carbon dioxide from your cells hitches onto the hemoglobin for the journey back to your lungs.

Did You Know?

Red blood cells survive for about four months in your blood. About 10 million RBCs die every second, but your body makes about 200 billion new ones every day.

Oxygen Overage

Pound for pound, seals have up to 50 percent more blood than people. And their red blood cells contain a lot more hemoglobin. Because seals can store so much oxygen in their blood, they can stay underwater for more than an hour. Most people can hold their breath for only about a minute.

A CAST OF COLORS

For every 15 white blood cells in your blood, there are about 250 platelets and more than 5,000 red blood cells. Most of the time, your body contains about 35 trillion RBCs. No wonder your blood is red!

Some other animals have red blood, too, but the liquid of life comes in a rainbow of colors.

Most of the time, a sea squirt's blood is apple green. But sometimes it turns blue or orange.

The bloodlike liquid flowing through the bodies of lobsters, crabs, snails, and shrimp is bluish green.

The blood of some sea worms is pink or violet.

Squids, octopuses, and horseshoe crabs have bright blue blood.

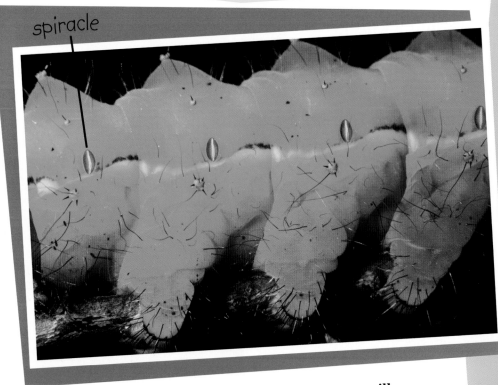

spiracle

A close up look at the spiracles of a caterpillar.

Insect Insides

An insect's circulatory system is different from yours. The colorless liquid flowing through its body transports nutrients and hormones, but not oxygen. That's because an insect doesn't have lungs or gills. It takes in air through **spiracles**, tiny holes on the sides of its body. Then a network of tubes carries the oxygen to all the insect's cells.

PLATELET PILEUP

Within seconds, masses of tiny platelets swarm the scene. They clump together and stick to the torn edges of broken blood vessels. And they keep piling up until they plug your cut and the bleeding stops.

Chemicals oozing out of the platelets mix with materials in the wounded area. They produce a web of tiny threads that strengthens your platelet plug.

As red blood cells whiz by, they get trapped in the web. They thicken your blood until a **clot** forms. After a few hours, the surface of the clot dries out. Then it hardens into a **scab** that protects your wound while it heals.

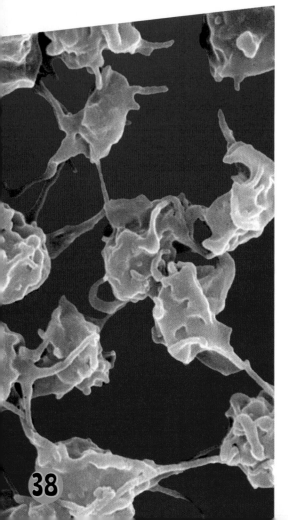

A close up view of platelets.

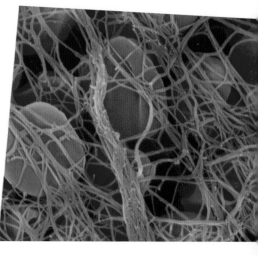

A blood clot as seen under a microscope

38

Platelet Production

Most platelets survive for about nine days in your blood. Luckily, your body is constantly cranking out a fresh supply. Like RBCs and WBCs, platelets are made in soft tissue at the center of the bones that support your back, chest, hips, arms, and legs.

Ick! Don't Pick!

You might be tempted to pick, poke, or prod a scab—but don't do it. Your body will have to start the healing process all over again. You might end up creating a **scar** that never goes away.

THE WHITE FIGHT

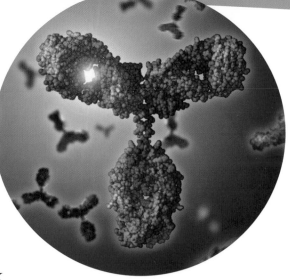

While a scab forms over the top of your cut, cells in the walls of the damaged blood vessels send out messages: "Help! Help!"

As your hardworking heart pumps blood through your body, more and more white blood cells flood the area of your cut. They track down tiny bits of dirt and gobble them up.

A human antibody.

And they chase down germs that have snuck into your wound.

But that's not all your WBCs do. They also attack germs that have entered your body in other ways. Some WBCs remember the invaders your body has fought in the past. If the same germ attacks again, these WBCs quickly crank out an army of **antibodies**—proteins that seek out and destroy a specific invader.

A white blood cell attacking debris.

From fighting germs and keeping our bodies at just the right temperature to supplying cells with food and oxygen, it's hard to believe all the ways our heart and blood help us every day. And we aren't alone. Other animals depend on them, too.

Signs of Trouble

• Have a cut that's red and swollen? That means germs and WBCs are battling it out.

• See a clump of goopy pus inside your wound? It's the piled-up bodies of dead WBCs. Yuck!

GLOSSARY

abdomen—In mammals, the section of the body that contains the stomach and intestines.

antibody—A protein that is programmed to find and destroy a specific germ.

artery—A blood vessel that carries blood away from the heart.

atrium (pl. atria)—One of the upper chambers of the heart. It receives blood from veins and arteries.

blood pressure—The pressure of the blood in the circulatory system. It is closely related to the force and rate of the heartbeat.

blood vessel—One of the tubes that carries blood throughout the body.

capillary—A tiny blood vessel through which oxygen and nutrients move into cells and carbon dioxide moves into the blood.

carbon dioxide—An invisible gas that animals make as they get energy from food.

circulatory system—The group of organs that transports blood throughout the body.

clot—A mass or lump. A blood clot is a mass of blood cells that can block a blood vessel. A dried clot on the surface of the skin is a scab.

consciousness—Awareness of being alive and understanding the world through the five senses.

digest—To break down food.

evaporate—To change from a liquid to a gas.

gill—A body part used by fish and some other animals that live in water to take in oxygen.

hemoglobin—The protein in red blood cells that carries oxygen molecules.

hormone—A substance that is produced in one part of the body and transported by blood to another part of the body, where it does a specific job.

mammal—A warm-blooded animal that has a backbone and feeds on its mother's milk. Almost all mammals have some hair or fur.

molecule—The smallest particle of a substance that retains the chemical and physical properties of the substance. A molecule is made of two or more atoms.

molt—To shed an old outer covering that is worn out or too small.

nutrient—A substance that comes from food and keeps the body healthy.

organ—A body part made up of several kinds of tissue that work together. The heart is an organ. So are the stomach and lungs.

oxygen—An invisible gas that animals need to live.

plasma—The liquid part of blood. It contains water, salts, nutrients, hormones, and waste products from cells.

platelet—A tiny cell fragment in the blood that helps close up cuts.

prey—An animal that is hunted by a predator.

protein—A molecule that speeds up chemical reactions (such as the steps of digestion), repairs damaged cells, ands builds new bones, teeth, hair, muscles, and skin.

pulse—The thumping you can feel in your neck or wrist when your heart beats.

red blood cell—A blood cell that delivers oxygen and nutrients to cells and transports carbon dioxide and other wastes away from cells.

scab—The dried remains of a blood clot. It acts as a protective covering until a wound heals.

scar—A mark left by a healed wound.

small intestine—The part of the digestive system that breaks down food particles and allows nutrients to pass into the blood.

spiracle—A small opening on the side of an insect through which air enters.

stethoscope—An instrument used to listen to a person's heartbeat.

vein—A blood vessel that carries blood toward the heart.

ventricle—One of the lower chambers of the heart. It receives blood from the atrium above it.

warm–blooded—Having a body temperature that stays the same no matter how cold or warm it is.

white blood cell—A blood cell that defends the body from germs and other invaders.

A NOTE ON SOURCES

Dear Readers,

I started my research for *Pump It Up!* by reading books about the human heart and blood but quickly realized that some of the information was out-of-date. I began relying more on recent magazine articles and research papers published in medical journals. I also searched for information on the Internet.

Some of the most interesting facts about the circulatory systems of other animals come from "And the Beat Goes On: A Brief Guide to the Hearts of Vertebrates" by Warren Burggren. That article appeared in the April 2000 issue of *Natural History* magazine. The information about the link between body size, heart rate, and life span comes from a report called "Size Matters: The Hidden Mathematics of Life." It was broadcast on National Public Radio on August 18, 2007.

When I had just about completed my research, I spoke with several doctors and scientists who are studying the circulatory system. Those interviews ensure that this book includes the most up-to-date information and statistics about the heart, blood flow, and blood cells.

—*Melissa Stewart*

FIND OUT MORE

BOOKS

Amazing Animals of the World. New York: Scholastic Library, 2006.

Brynie, Faith Hickman. *101 Questions About Blood and Circulation*. Minneapolis, MN: Twenty-First Century Books, 2001.

Oxlade, Chris. *The Circulatory System*. Chicago: World Book, Inc., 2007.

Romanek, Trudee. *Squirt! The Most Interesting Book You'll Ever Read About Blood*. Toronto, Ontario, Canada: Kids Can Press, 2006.

WEBSITES

The Giant Heart
This site gives an overview of the heart and its workings.
http://www.fi.edu/biosci/index.html

Guinness World Records
This site contains information on some of the strangest world's records you can imagine.
http://www.guinnessworldrecords.com/default.aspx

Kids Health
This site answers just about any question you might have about your body and keeping it healthy.
http://kidshealth.org/kid/

INDEX

Page numbers in **bold** are illustrations.

ABOUT THE AUTHOR

Melissa Stewart has written everything from board books for preschoolers to magazine articles for adults. She is the award-winning author of more than one hundred books for young readers. She serves on the board of advisors for the Society of Children's Book Writers and Illustrators and is a judge for the American Institute of Physics Children's Science Writing Award. Melissa earned a B.S. in biology from Union College and an M.A. in science journalism from New York University. She lives in Acton, Massachusetts, with her husband, Gerard. To learn more about Stewart, please visit her website: www.melissa-stewart.com.

ABOUT THE ILLUSTRATOR

Janet Hamlin has illustrated many children's books, games, newspapers and even Harry Potter stuff. She is also a court artist. Gross and Goofy is one of her all-time favorite series, and she now considers herself the factoid queen of bodily functions. She lives and draws in New York and loves it.